D1452200

THE AMERICAN COMMITTEE ON THE

COPYRIGHT 1883 BY THE AMERICAN BANK NOTE CO. NEW YORK

STATUE OF LIBERTY

PRESENTED BY THE

People of the Republic of France to the
People of the United States of America, hereby certify
that _____ has
contributed the sum of _____
to the fund for the erection of a suitable Pedestal for this Magnificent Monument.

Jos. W. Drexel CHAIRMAN.

Parke Godwin.

C. Mumford Moore

F. A. Coll

James W. Pinchot

EXECUTIVE COMMITTEE.

Wm. M. Evarts PRESIDENT.

Richard Butler SECRETARY.

Henry F. Spaulding TREASURER.

THE STATUE
OF LIBERTY
ENLIGHTENING
THE WORLD

THE STATUE
OF LIBERTY
ENLIGHTENING
THE WORLD

Frederic Auguste Bartholdi

New York Bound
New York

First published by North American Review in New York and copyrighted in 1885.

This facsimile edition published in 1984 by New York Bound,
43 West 54th Street, New York, N.Y. 10019.

Printed in the United States of America.

The reproduction of the engraving on the front cover is from Frank Leslie's
Popular Monthly, issued August, 1885.

The engraving of the Contribution Certificate in the front matter originally
appeared in *Inauguration of the Statue of Liberty Enlightening the World,*
D. Appleton & Co. (New York, 1887).

Library of Congress Cataloging in Publication Data

Bartholdi, Frédéric Auguste, 1834-1904.
   The Statue of Liberty enlightening the world.

   Reprint. Originally published: New York:
North American Review, 1885.
   1. Bartholdi, Frédéric Auguste, 1834-1904.
2. Statue of Liberty National Monument (New York, N.Y.)
3. New York (N.Y.)—Statues.   I. Title.
NB553.B3A4   1984   730'.92'4   84-1023
ISBN 0-9608788-6-6 (lim. ed.)
ISBN 0-9608788-5-8 (pbk.)

INTRODUCTION

This slim volume was written by Frederic Auguste Bartholdi on his own initiative in the Spring of 1885. It served two purposes: it helped to raise money for the American Pedestal Committee (Bartholdi in fact never received any payment for his work on the statue) and it gave the opportunity to the French sculptor to tell his own story of how he built the Statue of Liberty.

Throughout the construction of the Statue, Bartholdi was often maligned by the American press. In particular, *The New York Times* and *Scribner's Monthly* belittled his artistic abilities and the merits of the entire project. Many Americans were clearly embarrassed by the Statue's colossal size, symbolism and its ancient dress.

In the United States raising funds for the pedestal was an all-consuming task of the American Pedestal Committee. Publisher Joseph Pulitzer finally raised the last $100,000 by using his new newspaper, *The World*, as a clarion. Theatrical and artistic benefits brought in needed cash to pay for the Connecticut granite and the services of the immigrant Italian stonemasons who constructed the massive pedestal designed by architect Richard Hunt. Collection boxes were installed on the promenade of the new Brooklyn Bridge, on Wall Street, and on New York City's ferry boats. Subscribers who sent in a dollar or five dollars would receive a small metallic model of the Statue. This booklet cost 75¢ in 1885 and was published in a small edition. Few copies have survived.

Bartholdi's account appears more for the record: it is quite modest and straight forward. Its first person voice is accurate. But Bartholdi does become emotional and dogmatic on one issue. The sculptor had often been accused that his preliminary designs for a Suez Canal Lighthouse in 1869 were very similar to the design of what eventually became the Statue of Liberty. The Suez project had been rejected by the Khedive, Ismail Pasha, as too costly. The Suez Lighthouse model and the completed Statue of Liberty are indeed sisters in many ways but Bartholdi here confounds his critics by simply and categorically stating that he never thought of the first while creating the second.

To Bartholdi, the Liberty project was a personal committment of twenty-one years. His mother was the model for the face while the woman who modeled for the torso eventually became his wife. His obsession with the idea of the colossal gave him the super-human energy to create "Liberty Enlightening the World," the Statue of Liberty as we know her today.

There was probably never a sculptor who worked so hard to assure his sculpture's funding, placement, and completion. Literally, hundreds of thousands of people contributed to the French and American fund raising committees. A National Lottery was held in France to secure the project's completion. Bartholdi claims that no fewer than 300,000 curious onlookers saw the fabrication of the Statue at the foundry in Paris. Many of them bought postcards and fragments, stamped as a souvenir of the visit.

The Statue of Liberty has withstood nearly 100 years of sea, wind, salt and visitors. Several times she has had radical internal surgery: a new lighting system for the torch, an elevator and new stairways. Still her simple yet forceful form graces the gateway to the New World, New York City. Today, few immigrants clutch the ships' railings as they sail by this maritime giantess. She has become a tourist attraction, a symbolic bottle-green survivor of a century of an expanding America.

Nearly a century later, New Yorkers, and for that matter all people continue to fall in love with her. Bartholdi would be enlightened to know that his "daughter," as he called her, is still very much with us. At 98 she is receiving her most elaborate and extensive face lift, in hopes that she will continue to guide us with her light of Liberty.

JEFFREY EGER
March, 1984

The Statue of Liberty Enlightening The World.

Described by the Sculptor BARTHOLDI

Published for the Benefit of the Pedestal Fund

BY THE

NORTH AMERICAN REVIEW

30 LAFAYETTE PLACE,

NEW YORK.

THE STATUE

OF

LIBERTY ENLIGHTENING THE WORLD

DESCRIBED BY THE SCULPTOR,

FREDERIC AUGUSTE BARTHOLDI.

———◦———

PUBLISHED FOR THE BENEFIT OF THE PEDESTAL FUND.

———◦———

North American Review,

30 LAFAYETTE PLACE,

NEW YORK.

After M. Bartholdi had written and sent the manuscript of this little book, he received from the dying Victor Hugo the following autograph, sent by the illustrious poet to be incorporated with it. They were probably the last words ever written by the greatest man-of-letters of his age:

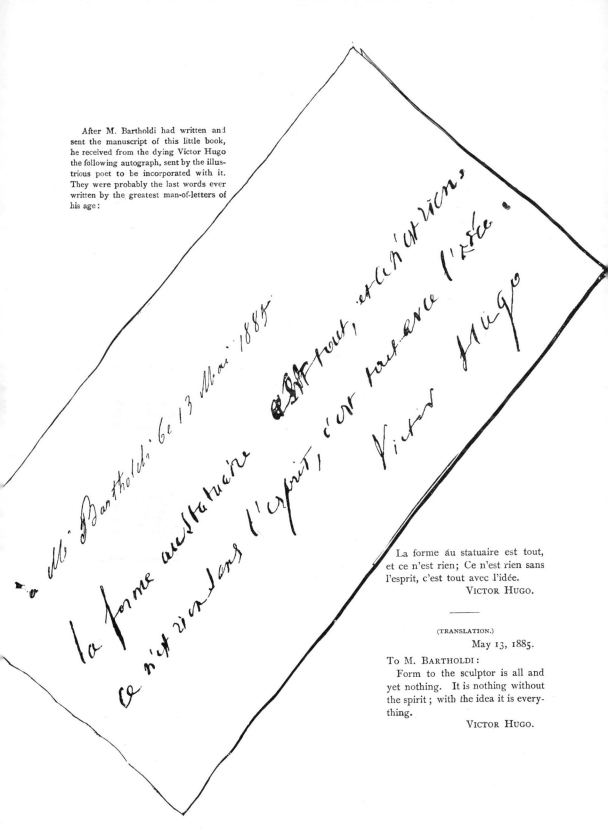

La forme áu statuaire est tout, et ce n'est rien; Ce n'est rien sans l'esprit, c'est tout avec l'idée.

VICTOR HUGO.

───────

(TRANSLATION.)

May 13, 1885.

To M. BARTHOLDI:

Form to the sculptor is all and yet nothing. It is nothing without the spirit; with the idea it is everything.

VICTOR HUGO.

ACKNOWLEDGMENT.

Cordial acknowledgment is hereby made to the AMERICAN BANK NOTE COMPANY for the use of the steel frontispiece, and to HARPER AND BROTHERS, the CENTURY COMPANY, D. APPLETON AND COMPANY, and the publishers of the *Scientific American,* for their kindness in contributing many of the wood cuts with which this little work is illustrated.

PREFATORY NOTE.

The object of this monograph by M. Bartholdi needs little further explanation than it carries in its own reading. Certainly the great American public will warmly sympathize with a publication which, aside from its unique value as a modest but bright little essay by a great sculptor on his own immortal work, will help to swell the fund so tardy in its accumulation, till the energy of a leading journal gave it fresh life.

In addition, however, to the pedestal fund proper, a further amount is needed, according to the statement of the committee, to provide for the cost of erecting the statue in place, for which Congress failed to make the expected appropriation. It is with this end in view that the following pages are offered to the public.

The career of M. Bartholdi, the most distinguished living sculptor of colossal statuary, bears testimony to the genius and unselfish industry which fashioned the Monument to Liberty. Born at Colmar in 1833, like some of his predecessors in the plastic art, he started life as a painter. Though apprenticed to the famous Ary Scheffer, M. Bartholdi, following a natural bent, soon turned his attention to sculpture, and produced, at the early age of 19, a notable bas-relief of Francesca da Rimini. From that time forward his fame has grown with the years. Like the battle painters de Neuville and Detaille, M. Bartholdi became inspired by the bloody Franco-German conflict, and produced in 1878 the Lion of Belfort, a colossal monument to the heroism of a beleaguered garrison, carved in the solid rock. A plaster cast of this great work, together with his statue "Gribeauval," now the property of the French nation, were, in 1878, among the chief attractions of the Paris Salon.

The Government bestowed on the sculptor the Cross of the Legion of Honor, and at the Centennial Exhibition he was awarded the medal for sculpture for a remarkable exhibit of an early but powerful work termed "Genius in the Grasp of Misery," and the later productions, "Peace," and "The Young Vine-Grower," all in bronze. Among his other important works may be named, "Vercingetorix," the old Gallic patriot, the graceful statue of "Lafayette" now standing in Union Square, New York, and three tributes to his native town, a fountain dedicated in 1863 to the memory of Martin Schongauer, the painter, a statue of Admiral Brouat, and one of General Rapp.

In the face of great difficulties, M. Bartholdi has, for over ten years, struggled manfully to see his gigantic work erected on the threshold of the new world. And it may be well here to state that his labor has been, from the outset, a labor of love and not of profit. For strange though it may seem, the sculptor has derived no pecuniary benefit from his arduous task. In a recent letter to the writer, he declares that for long years he has made many serious sacrifices of time and money, in consummating this great life-purpose. But, if the burden has been hard to bear, he has found his reward. In consecrating a tribute to Liberty, he has fashioned the eighth wonder of the world.

A. T. R.

The Statue of Liberty.

HISTORY OF THE WORK OF THE FRENCH-AMERICAN UNION.*

The account which I have been asked to prepare of the work of the French-American Union, of its history and its accomplishment, is a somewhat delicate thing for me to do, because of the difficulty of treating properly a subject in which I am obliged often to speak of myself. Apart from this consideration, however, I willingly accept the task of preparing this account, because it allows me to rectify many errors and to give correct information to those interested in this question.

If, then, the reader sees the "I" or the "me" appear frequently, he will excuse me. It will be the narrative form alone that will be the cause of it, and he will understand that I have no desire to speak of myself, and will see that the "me" appears only as much as is necessary for the development of the subject which I am to treat.

* Under the name of the French-American Union is designated in France the society which has undertaken the carrying out of the plan of the colossal Statue of Liberty.

2

The origin of the work of the French-American Union is of so modest a character that it would be very difficult to search it out if I did not recount it myself. That makes necessary a little recital of some circumstances in my own life.

One evening, twenty years ago, I had been dining at the home of my most regretted and illustrious friend, M. Laboulaye, and his guests were smoking in the conservatory of his charming retreat, Glavigny, near Versailles. It was a gathering of men eminent in politics and letters. The talk fell upon international relations, upon the sentiments of Italy toward France. Some one said that gratitude could not exist among nations, that the least material interest, that the lightest political breath, would break every tie of that sort; coming to the United States, the remark was added that France could no more count on the remembrance of the past.

M. Laboulaye observed, that in the case of Italy there had never been a popular tradition of friendship; that in 1859 a service had been done her, but she had been made to feel that France had repaid herself for it; and that fact was sufficient to make the remembrance unpleasant to the Italians. It was a wholly different thing in the case of other nations or peoples with whom there was a genuine flow of sympathy, caused, it might be, by experiences common to the two nations, it might be by affinity of aspiration, or by the influence of certain feelings which served as a bond of union.

Coming to the American Nation, he said that it had more sympathy for France than for any other European nation; that this sentiment did not bear the stamp of gratitude, but was based upon the remembrance of the community of thoughts and of struggles, sustained with common aspirations. The Frenchmen who fought in the United States spilled their blood for the principles that they hoped to see prevail in France and in the world. The first volunteers went away in spite of the Government, and all the world recalls the difficulties encountered by Lafayette at his departure. There is then, he said, in that struggle for independence, not a simple service rendered to a friendly nation, but a fraternity of feelings, a community of efforts and of emotions; and when hearts have beaten together something always remains among nations as among individuals.

The proof, he added, is that in the United States they hold up to honor the remembrance of the common glories, they love Lafayette and his volunteers as they revere the American heroes. In the public mind this remembrance is much clearer than that of the political action of the French Government. No one in the United

States speaks of the Treaty of Versailles, which made the United States what they are. Many Americans are ignorant even of the date of that treaty. On the other hand, every one recalls the names and the deeds of the French soldiers. There, said M. Laboulaye, is the basis of the sentiments which are felt in the United States toward the French, an indestructible basis, a sentiment honorable to the Americans as to us, and if a monument were to be built in America as a memorial to their independence, I should think it very natural if it were built by united effort, if it were a common work of both nations.

I cite these words from memory, since they have never been put in print so far as I know; but this conversation interested me so deeply that it remained fixed in my memory, and if I am not able to give the precise form of it, at least the ideas are exact, because they may be found in the addresses of M. Laboulaye in regard to the work of the French-American Union.

This conversation came back to my mind a long time afterward, at the period of the war of 1870. I was with the army in the East, where we struggled for long ·months against the enemy and against our severe sufferings, always hopeful, always with faith in the future.

I was sent to· Bordeaux to get some arms and munitions which came from America on board of the vessels of the Transatlantic Company. It was with pain that I heard the officers of the vessel speak of the demonstrations in the United States in favor of Germany. One of them, however, defended the Americans. He said those clamorous demonstrations were the work of Germans who had been in America only a short time; that those who had been long in the United States respected the traditions of their new country; that the greater part of them remembered how they had been ground under foot, condemned to death, obliged to fly from their native land, when they had dreamed of possessing some liberties, of enjoying equality; that those who rejoiced over the success of Germany rejoiced rather in the fact of a United Germany, and in the hope of seeing that unity result in the political and social development of their former country, for the happiness of their relatives and friends who remained therein; but that these very men were too much Americans and citizens of the great free people to feel hatred toward France or to rejoice over the misfortunes of the nation which helped to create their new country, whose· prosperity they enjoy to-day.

All those comments, those varied opinions, excited my lively interest. I had always felt a sympathetic curiosity concerning America, and a lively desire to know the country.

When the war was over I could not go to my native land, Alsace, which was shut against me by the Germans; at Paris, the Commune was in power and civil war was raging. After a short stay in Switzerland, I resolved to take a journey in order to withdraw myself from all the painful impressions of the year through which I had just passed, and the idea came to me of going to visit America.

I went to Versailles to see again the friends whom I had not seen for so many dolorous months; I found myself again at the house of M. Laboulaye, with Messieurs Lafayette, Henri Martin, Rémusat, Volowski, de Gasparin and other distinguished men, whose sympathies toward the United States were well known. They talked again of American sentiment, of the shipments which the Americans had made to Paris, of the diverse opinions which prevailed in America. I repeated all that I had heard said on board of the Transatlantic steamships. M. Laboulaye took up again his views as expressed previously, and declared that without any doubt there would be at the hundredth anniversary of the Independence of the United States a movement patriotic and French in America. "Go to see that country," said he to me. "You will study it, you will bring back to us your impressions. Propose to our friends over there to make with us a monument, a common work, in remembrance of the ancient friendship of France and the United States. We will take up a subscription in France. If you find a happy idea, a plan that will excite public enthusiasm, we are convinced that it will be successful on both continents, and we will do a work that will have a far-reaching moral effect."

It was, then, in these convictions of M. Laboulaye, that the germ of the monument of the French-American Union was found.

I have related these fragments of conversation, in order that they may show how the idea had its birth and development; but I do it still more to answer those who, with an evil spirit of disparagement, have desired to diminish the value of the work by treating it as the personal fantasy of an artist. I may fairly claim a certain merit in the invention of the idea, in working it out and in carrying the undertaking to completion; but it has a value greater than that; it has roots deeper than an artist's ambition.

The popular subscription in France has shown it, and Messieurs Laboulaye, Lafayette, De Tocqueville, De Lasteyrie and others foresaw that depth of public sentiment when they said, that if a method of stirring up the public in the two countries, by means of some thrilling suggestion, some sound and luminous idea, could be found, the success which would follow would astonish every one.

Above all, then, should be honored those faithful friends of the United States, who have shown in this matter their faith and their enthusiasm. This is the moment, if ever, to recall them to mind. Alas! they are no longer here to see the accomplishment of the work, but, before leaving us, they saw the certainty of success, and their benediction will accompany the Statue of Liberty.

Imbued with the thoughts of those eminent men, furnished with their letters of recommendation, enjoying full authority to express myself or to engage myself in their names, I departed for America.

In the course of the voyage I formed some conceptions of a plan of a monument, but I can say that at the view of the harbor of New York the definite plan was first clear to my eyes.

The picture that is presented to the view when one arrives at New York is marvelous; when, after some days of voyaging, in the pearly radiance of a beautiful morning is revealed the magnificent spectacle of those immense cities, of those rivers extending as far as the eye can reach, festooned with masts and flags; when one awakes, so to speak, in the midst of that interior sea covered with vessels, some giants in size, some dwarfs, which swarm about, puffing, whistling, swinging the great arms of their uncovered walking-beams, moving to and fro like a crowd upon

VIEW OF THE HARBOR OF NEW YORK FROM FORT RICHMOND.

From Appleton's "New York Illustrated."

a public place. It is thrilling. It is, indeed, the New World, which appears in its majestic expanse, with the ardor of its glowing life. Was it not wholly natural that the artist was inspired by this spectacle? Yes, in this very place shall be raised the Statue of Liberty, grand as the idea which it embodies, radiant upon the two worlds. If, then, the form of the accomplished work is mine, to the

3

Americans I owe the thought and the inspiration which gave it birth. I was conscious when I landed at New York that I had found the idea which my friends had hoped for.

The second part of my mission remained to be accomplished; to learn if the dream could become a reality. For that it was necessary at the outset to Americanize myself a little, to become acquainted with the country, the persons and the things, to become familiar with all the difficulties in order to hit upon the means of triumphant success.

I traveled from the East to the West, from the North to the South, and visited nearly all the great cities of the United States and a great number of little ones that have, perhaps, become very great ones which I should not now recognize. In short, I made an artistic journey through the cities, and through the wild regions as well, painting and designing, finding acquaintances everywhere; and I employed my time so well for five months that I brought back a more general knowledge of the United States than many Americans possess.

As to acquaintance with the world and with individuals, I received a speedy initiation, thanks to the distinguished men whom I had the honor of knowing; they were perhaps the cause that I am reproached everywhere for my excessive partiality for Americans. I retain always in lively remembrance the welcome that I received in the course of this first journey, and the friendship with which I was honored by men who are illustrious everywhere. I shall always recall Longfellow, who received me as if he had always known me, who, when I left him, pressed my hand as if he wished electrically to convey that pressure to his friends in France, charging me to express to them all his enthusiasm for their plans. It gave me so much pleasure to see that noble figure, that several times I made the journey to Boston to pass some hours there.

In speaking of noble faces, there was another which impressed me much, that of Senator Sumner. I was in his company often at Washington. I was filled with admiration of his intellectual power, of the fineness of his spirit, and his working faculties. I went to pass the evening at his house, interrupting him in his labors, and then with extraordinary animation he told me a hundred charming anecdotes, he questioned me about a thousand things in French politics or letters that he was far better acquainted with than I. I saw him for the last time at Paris; I had the pleasure of taking him to the home of Gambetta, whom he desired to know; they had a long conversation, lasting more than an hour, and of the liveliest interest. I shall always remember the last words of Mr. Sumner, who in going out, inclining his majestic figure, said with a meaning smile: "My dear M. Gambetta, I shall always believe that it was a great misfortune for France that Henry Fourth coined so neat a phrase to take the city of Paris."*

But I perceive that I let myself wander away too easily, and play truant when I think of the persons whom I had the pleasure of meeting in that first journey.

I have of necessity seen much of the world, and some strong friendships remain to me, a product, as it were, of the moral freemasonry which rules in humanity, and brings it about that certain persons enter into each other's thoughts at the outset, as if they had known each other for a long time.

I stopped to speak of those two men, the honor and boast of the United States, because it was delightful to me to call up the remembrance of them, and to bring to them the tribute of my respect in recalling the sympathy with which they honored me.

Among the notabilities to whom I had the honor of being presented I will mention General Grant, President of the United States at that time, General Meade, General Sheridan, Mr. Peter Cooper, Mr. Cyrus Field, Mr. Agassiz, Colonel Forney and other members of the press. All the

---

* When he became a Catholic, saying: "Paris is well worth a mass."

names are no longer in my recollection. I received a most cordial welcome at the Union League Club in New York and in Philadelphia. Finally, the kindness with which I was welcomed everywhere showed the profound consideration enjoyed by my eminent fellow-countrymen under whose auspices I had come to the United States.

It was not very difficult for me to establish a good understanding on which to lay the foundations of the plan of my Parisian friends. I had made a sketch in water-colors of the monument of Liberty on Bedloe's Island, and after becoming assured among my kindly approving friends of the impression that the plan would produce, I acquired the certainty that when we should begin in France the United States would second us, and that the draft drawn by Messieurs Laboulaye, Lafayette, Henri Martin and their friends upon American sentiments would not be protested.

On my return, M. Laboulaye called together his friends at his house. I imparted the results of my journey, my impressions, the welcome that I had received, the co-laborers upon whom we could count, and I presented the plan of the monument which I had made.

M. Henri Martin (whose place in the Academy has just been filled by the illustrious De Lesseps) spoke of that reunion in an official address. I quote his words, in spite of the praises which they contain, because it is necessary for me to show the warmth of the sentiments which were manifested on that occasion:

> It was needful for us to discover a thought in harmony with the object to be attained. The artist presented it to us in a form that bore the stamp of genius. He had conceived the celebration of the anniversary of Independence, applying to it a sublime phrase which sums up the progress of modern times: " Liberty Enlightening the World."
>
> M. Bartholdi proposed to represent this great idea by a statue of colossal proportions which would surpass all that have ever existed since the most ancient times.
>
> We adopted this plan with enthusiasm. A committee was organized. Artists, public men, constituted bodies, general councils, municipal councils and chambers of commerce associated themselves in the enterprise, and the movement which had started from so modest an origin became a genuine national demonstration.
>
> HENRI MARTIN, *May 27,* 1879.

I will not enter upon the detailed recital of all that the committee did; I will confine myself to recalling the main points which marked their action.

The plan of the French-American Union was not launched upon the public until the end of the year 1874. Up to that time it had been organized, the means had been prepared, and I had made the first models. [See note A.]

Subscription lists were circulated throughout France at that time. They bore at the head the following, prepared by Mr. Laboulaye:

The Monument of Independence will be executed in common by the two peoples associated in this fraternal work, as they were of old in establishing Independence. In this way we declare by an imperishable memorial the friendship that the blood spilled by our fathers of old sealed between the two nations. It is a treaty of friendship which should be signed by all hearts which feel the love of their country.

E. LABOULAYE.

The appeal had a considerable response. The birth of the work was celebrated on November 6, 1875, in the Hotel of the Louvre by a banquet which has remained memorable. The arts, letters, the press, politics, sent there illustrious representatives both from America and from France.

In that hall, whose echoes repeated again and again the names of Franklin and of Washington, were seen near each other the representatives of the names of Lafayette and of Rochambeau.

Near Mr. Washburne, Minister Plenipotentiary from the United States, near Mr. Forney, Commissioner-General in Europe of the Universal Exposition of the same States, were seen the members of the originating committee: Messieurs Laboulaye, Henri Martin, Dietz Mounir, Oscar de Lafayette, Jules de Lasteyrie, Paul de Rémusat, Waddington, Count Sérurier, Cornélis de Witt, Jean Macé, Victor Borie, Caubert, A. Bartholdi, de Lagorsse, de Tocqueville, Viollet-Leduc, Volowski.

That banquet brought together men of all opinions; the chief Ministers, Deputies, the Aide-de-camp and the Secretary of the President of the Republic, the President of the Municipal Council of Paris, American and French Generals, Academicians, Authors, Savants and Journalists representing all varieties and all shades of politics.

The success of the work was assured. To raise the necessary funds there were festivals and exhibitions. The illustrious author of " Faust," Gounod, had composed a hymn for the Statue of Liberty. It was sung at the opera, and M. Laboulaye held a conference. Going upon the stage he said to his friends : " See how much I love the Americans! At my great age I mount the platform for them." [See notes.]

To give at that time in America an idea of the work, the right hand of the statue was executed in its colossal proportions and sent to the Exposition at Philadelphia.

I returned to the United States at that period as a member of the French Jury. In the same year took place in New York the inauguration of the statue of Lafayette, with the execution of which I had been intrusted by the French Government, and which was presented to the city in acknowledgment of the sympathy New York had testified to France by her numerous shipments at the time of the sufferings caused by the siege of Paris.

These circumstances, which awaken patriotic feelings, gave an opportunity for getting the American public earnestly interested in the grand project of their French friends. A preparatory meeting was organized at the Century Club upon the call of W. M. Evarts, S. D. Babcock, John Jay, W. H. Wickham, William H. Appleton and Richard Butler, Secretary.

At that meeting a committee was organized and a memorial was addressed to the Government of the United States, asking approval and support for what had been done by the French concerning the site of the monument.

Congress on the 22d of February, 1877, voted in favor of accepting the gift of France and setting apart Bedloe's Island for the site, in terms most flattering to the work and to the French nation. [See note B.]

When I came back to France the taking of subscriptions was going on actively. I executed the head of the statue for the Paris Exposition of 1878. In the following year all the funds necessary for the execution of the statue were obtained. On July 7, 1880, the sending of the official notification to the American Committee of the progress of the work and of the date when the labors upon it would be completed, was celebrated by a fête given to General Noyes, the United States Minister at Paris. This notification was sent to the United States upon an

UNITED STATES MINISTER MORTON DRIVING THE FIRST RIVET IN THE PEDESTAL.

From *Harper's Weekly*, Dec. 3, 1881.

illuminated parchment signed by the members of the Committee and all the Frenchmen who were present.

The work of execution made rapid progress. On October 24, 1881, the anniversary of the battle of Yorktown, all the pieces of the framework and of the base were put in place. The Committee invited Mr. Morton, who was the new United States Minister at that time, to come and drive the rivet of the first piece which was to be mounted. It was the left foot of the statue.

Mr. Morton was cordially greeted by a numerous assemblage, and M. Laboulaye bade him welcome. This ceremony left a strong impression on everyone, and it echoed through the country.

The work on the statue was carried on from that time without slackening and with a numerous force. It was constantly visited by the public, who showed a lively interest in it. It is estimated that about 300,000 persons visited the workshops.

The statue was nearly finished in 1883; but as the work on the pedestal was not far enough advanced to permit of its erection, it was decided to leave it for some time exposed to view in Paris.

On June 11, 1884, at a great dinner given by Mr. Morton to the Committee of the French-American Union and to the Ministers of the French Government, M. Ferry,

OVER THE HOUSETOPS OF PARIS.

From *Harper's Weekly*, August 9, 1884.

President of the Council, announced that the Government had followed with the liveliest interest the progress of this work, which had been accomplished completely outside the range of its influence and by the energy of the private persons who had initiated it. He found that it was time for the Government to associate itself with the undertaking, and the colossal Statue of Liberty presented to the Americans would be transported to New York on a State vessel under the official banner of France.

M. de Lesseps, who had been called to the presidency of the Committee after the death of our dear and illustrious friend, M. Laboulaye, replied in most happy terms. He finished his address by proposing to appoint the official delivery of the Statue of Liberty to the United States Minister for the Fourth of July, and to deliver it in the presence of M. Ferry and the Ministers of the French Government.

The President of the Council willingly accepted the suggestion, and thus the ceremony which brilliantly crowned all the work of the Society of the French-American Union was decided upon. [See notes B, C and D, for the details.]

After the date of that ceremony, the statue remained exposed to public view, and the people continued to pour out to visit it until January 1, 1885. At that time the work of taking it down was begun. This was performed with great care, all the pieces being marked according to a classification which was simple and easy to follow.

At the present hour the whole work is packed up in 210 cases which in a few days are to be put on board the State vessel Isére at Rouen. They will arrive in the United States toward the end of May.*

Such is the succinct presentation of the work of the French-American Union. In order to complete this account it remains for me to give some explanation of the artistic features and the processes of the material execution.

* M. Bartholdi, it should be remembered by the reader, wrote this article about May 1st. There was some delay about the sailing of the Isére.

Colossal Sculpture.

THE PRINCIPAL EXAMPLES OF THIS CLASS—THE METHODS OF
EXECUTION EMPLOYED ON THE STATUE OF LIBERTY.

I think that it may be timely to examine briefly the characteristics of colossal statuary, in view of the fact that the art has from time to time been the object of criticism. Many persons see in it only a striking production, and do not understand its peculiar laws, its difficulties, nor its artistic value.

Colossal statuary does not consist simply in making an enormous statue. It ought to produce an emotion in the breast of the spectator, not because of its volume, but because its size is in keeping with the idea that it interprets, and with the place which it ought to occupy. It should be used only in dealing with a limited order of ideas. M. Lesbazeilles, in his work on the Colossi, has said with reason: "It is within its scope when it represents power, majesty, infinity. It can lay claim to that

FULL VIEW OF
THE STATUE OF LIBERTY
AS IT STOOD IN PARIS.

—

From *Harper's Weekly*,
June 19, 1884.

THE FLAME.

THE FOOT.

class of effects which are produced in us by the heaving of the boundless sea, the bellowing of the wind, the rolling of the thunder."

Also M. Charles Blanc, the celebrated art critic, says on the same subject:

> Colossal statuary calls for faculties of peculiar power. It is an art of an exceptional character, which presents considerable difficulties. The artist who approaches these difficulties enters a sombre temple, peopled with mysteries. He is brought face to face with struggles which few artists have experienced. No one can advise him, nothing can guide him except his instinct, his faith and his courage. Conception and execution are controlled by rigid and difficult laws. Faults once committed can be hidden by no subterfuge, and if the artist fails the depth of his fall is commensurate with the immensity of his aspirations. Instead of producing many works in which he may attain success in a variety of ways, he exhausts a large part of his life upon a single task, on which he pours out all his treasures of passion, of study and of enthusiasm. With these he must without pause keep up his ardor during long years.—CHARLES BLANC in *Le Temps*.

These words seem to me to answer in a large measure the criticisms of which colossal art is sometimes the object.

Without wishing to make a detailed study of the colossal statues which have been produced, I think that it might be interesting to the reader to recall rapidly the most remarkable works of this kind of past times. Egypt incontestably gives us on this point the most complete instruction, and we can judge Egyptian colossal art with our own eyes.

5

To all those who have studied it, Egyptian art has been the object of profound admiration, not only in view of the masses, the millions of kilogrammes moved by the Egyptian people, but on account of its concrete and majestic character, in design and in form, of the works which we see. We are filled with profound emotion in presence of these colossal witnesses, centuries old, of a past that to us is almost infinite, at whose feet so many generations, so many million existences, so many human glories, have rolled in the dust. These granite beings, in their imperturbable majesty, seem to be still listening to the most remote antiquity. Their kindly and impassable glance seems to ignore the present and to be fixed upon an unlimited future. These impressions are not the result simply of a beautiful spectacle, nor of the poetry of historic remembrances. They result from the character of the form and the expression of the work in which the design itself expresses after a fashion infinity.

I have studied Egyptian art with the greatest attention. When I was twenty years old I traveled in Egypt with the painters Gerome and Belly, and several other friends, and I may say that this country had a very considerable effect upon my taste for sculpture of the broad and decorative type. In 1868 I went back with M. de Lesseps and gazed again with the same pleasure on all those marvellous ruins, and my convictions grew stronger upon the principles which are there to be discovered.*

Assyrian art also presents specimens of colossal sculpture of the finest kind, only its effect is less striking because the finest remaining types of this art are in bas-reliefs. The taste for colossal art certainly made its way into Greece along with many other artistic traditions which came from Assyria, as well as from Egypt. Archæologists have often asserted this relationship. Phidias executed two colossal statues, in which he succeeded in uniting material grandeur with a true ideal of beauty of form. The statue of Minerva in the Parthenon measured thirty-seven feet, and that of the Olympian Jove forty feet. They have both been regarded as masterpieces of chrys-elephantine sculpture (otherwise called sculpture in gold and ivory). All the ancient authors, Pausanias, Pliny, Quintilian, have spoken of them with much enthusiasm, and in terms which leave no doubt of the value of those works, and of the profound impression which they produced on the Grecian

* At this period I was expecting to execute a statue of Egypt for the Suez Lighthouse. I even laid before Ismail Pacha a project. It was this that made an evilly disposed newspaper say, and others repeat, that I had executed a colossal statue for Egypt, which had not been used, and that I had resold it to the Society of the French-American Union in order that from it might be made the Statue of Liberty.

Now, I never executed anything for the Khedive except a little sketch which has remained in his palace, and represents Egypt under the features of a female Fellah. Besides every one has seen the model of the Statue of Liberty made at Paris, and only evilly disposed persons are ignorant of what it has cost me. I have never answered these small cavilings, but I think that I ought to notice them on this occasion.

world. The other admired works of that period which have come down to us permit us to consider them good judges.

The most celebrated colossal statue of antiquity was the Colossus of Rhodes. We may consider it as having been a very remarkable piece of work, independently of the fantastic legend of the ships which passed between its outspread legs. This legend, whose origin is not older than the sixteenth century, has been exploded by arch-æologists; nevertheless we may add to the observations a demonstration founded on simple good sense. First, If the Colossus was placed with its legs apart above the water, when it was overthrown it would have fallen into the water, and the enormous fragments, resembling caverns, of which Pliny speaks, would not have been gotten out, leaving within the stones, themselves enormous, which he says he saw there. Second, The result of my personal studies shows that the placing of a statue of this kind in an upright position would be almost impossible, but that it would be absolutely so if stones were placed in the body, which would result in bringing the centre of gravity too high.

After the Grecian epoch we must pass on to modern times to find examples of colossal statues. The Jupiter Pluvius of the Pratolino Villa, executed by John of Bologna,

and the St. Charles Borromeo on the banks of Lake Mag-
giore, may be referred to. It cannot be said that this last
work is properly included under the head of colossal art.
It is an ordinary statue enlarged, and its volume gives it
its principal interest. The pedestal is deplorable, and nothing in the whole work shows either research into the
principles of colossal art or a comprehension of them.
Nevertheless this work of art has a peculiar interest in
virtue of its material execution. It is, I think, the first
example of the use of repoussé copper mounted on iron
trusses. In ancient times metal beaten out into sheets had
already been used. But it was used as a covering or was
modeled on a solid form of wood or stone. Gold, silver
and copper were thus employed in Grecian antiquity and
in the extreme Orient. The statue of St. Charles Borromeo
is the first known example of a statue of répoussé copper,
worked with the hammer inside and outside, and freely
supported on iron beams. The work was executed in a
somewhat coarse style, but it is interesting, and has the
merit of being the result of a bold initiative. The copper
is a little thin, measuring only a millimetre in thickness,
and yet the whole work has stood until to-day, that is to
say, for two centuries.

All the other colossal statues in existence are entirely
modern. That of Bavaria is the oldest. It measures 15.70

metres. Next was executed the colossal statue of the
Virgin of Puy, which is 16 metres in height; and finally
that of Arminius in Westphalia which, including the sword
which he raises toward the sky, is 28.30 metres in height.

The object of this review of the colossal statues which
have been produced up to the present time, is to bring
back their image to our eyes, and to enable us to deduce
from them some principles which seem to be essential in
colossal art. The understanding of these principles and
their interpretation may vary somewhat according to the
sentiments of the artist. Yet some of them seem to me
to manifest themselves in a way which admits of no dis-
cussion. They are to be found:

1st—In the character or the thought of the subject,
which ought to be in harmony with the size of the work.

2d—In the suitableness of the site and the surround-
ings of the monument.

3d—In the understanding of the lines and the make-
up which, in colossal works of art, are rendered necessary
by the execution.

On the first point I will recall the words of M. Lesbazeilles, which I cited above, when he says that colossal
statuary ought to be used only to symbolize figures of
thoughts which are grand in themselves, and as far as
possible, abstract. The immensity of form should be filled

with the immensity of thought, and the spectator, at the sight of the great proportions of the work, should be impressed, before all things else, with the greatness of the idea of which these ample forms are the envelope, without being obliged to have recourse to comparative measurements in order to feel himself moved.

In regard to the choice of site, a study should be made of similar existing works in order clearly to perceive the most favorable conditions. The frame should lend itself to the subject. It may be made upon improved architectural effects, by the flights of stairs which lead up to the statue and contribute to the monumental character, but above all a site favorable by its own nature should be sought. There is an instinct which ought to guide the artist, for he ought to turn Nature to account in such a way as to make her contribute to the aspect of the monument. The neighborhood of large masses should be avoided. The artist ought to choose his site in such a way that the lines of the ground and the coloring of the background will become his assistants in heightening the proper appearance of his work and the impression which it is to produce.

In regard to the execution of colossal works of art, I think, as I said above, that we find sure principles in the ancient works. The difficulty is to apply them to one's own age, that is to say, without servile imitation of the forms imagined by other epochs and other races.

I may cite for example the principle of great simplicity in the movement and in the exterior lines. The gesture ought to be made plain by the profile to all the senses. The details of the lines ought not to arrest the eye. The breaks in the lines should be bold, and such as are suggested by the general design. Beside the work should be as far as possible filled out, and should not present black spots or exaggerated recesses. The surfaces should be broad and simple, defined by a bold and clear design, accentuated in the important places. The enlargement of the details or their multiplicity is to be feared. By exaggerating the forms, in order to render them more clearly visible, or by enriching them with details, we would destroy the proportion of the work. Finally, the model, like the design, should have a summarized character, such as one would give to a rapid sketch. Only it is necessary that this character should be the product of volition and study, and that the artist, concentrating his knowledge, should find the form and the line in its greatest simplicity.

These same principles ought to be kept in mind in the construction of the pedestal, for they exist in architecture. I could, if I were not afraid of being prolix, cite examples of remarkable edifices, in which the enlargement of certain details, or the lack of simplicity in the lines, prevent the spectator from appreciating at first sight the monumental proportions of the edifice.

These are subjects on which there might be much said. I thought that it would be well to touch lightly upon them, not with the pretension of laying down principles, but to show the thoughts which animated me, the artistic considerations and the ideals by which I have sought to be guided in my work.

THE WORK ON THE STATUE.

Up to the present time no statue had ever been exe-. cuted of the extraordinary proportions of the Statue of Liberty. In order to form an idea of this work, which was without precedent, it was necessary to give the greatest attention to the means of execution; it was necessary to foresee the elements of solidity and the exigencies of transportation to America; finally, it was necessary to seek to avoid heavy expenses, into which one is rapidly drawn in a work of this kind, according to the methods employed. The examination of the various difficulties led us to adopt the system of hammered copper, which, from an artistic point of view, offers elements of excellence when it is well treated, which allows of a large subdivision in the pieces, and renders the transportation easy.

We will examine the various phases of the work. The total height of the first model was 1.25 metres. This was the study model, which was long sought and often recast.

MODELING THE HEAD.
From *St. Nicholas*, July, 1884.

(It is the model which has been reproduced in terra-cotta, the number of the reproductions being limited to two hundred. Each model was numbered and registered, and a large number of them were sold in aid of the subscription under the name of the "Model of the Committee.")

After this first study I made the statue which measures from the head to the feet 2.8 metres, and in its entirety 2.85 metres. This statue, executed with rigid precision, was reproduced four times as large by the ordinary processes. The model which was the result of this work measured about 11 metres in total height. Placed in a large space it could be taken in by the eye in its entirety, and the corrections to be made could still be noted. This statue was divided into a large number of sections destined to be reproduced separately at four times their size. After this last enlargement

AT WORK ON THE LEFT HAND.
From *St. Nicholas*, July, 1884.

changes were no longer possible. Now the sculptor could only aim at very great precision, and at great care in the

modeling of the surfaces, which were becoming enormous.
It was necessary to study them in their simplicity and their
nakedness, so that the form should be flowing and correct,
without prominent details, which would detract from the
general appearance. In an immense workshop, specially
constructed for the work, were to be seen four plane surfaces
on which the work was carried on. They were encom-
passed with frames laid out in numbered divisions. Another
similar frame, corresponding exactly to the one below, was
fastened beneath the ceiling of the workshop. Lead wires
and rulers hung all around the frames. On these frames,
thus geometrically laid out, the sculptors executed, in wood
and in plaster, enormous fragments of the statue. The
sections of the model that they were to reproduce were
arranged near by under corresponding conditions, between
frames of one-fourth the size. The sculptors executed the
enlargement by measurements taken with the compass on
the lead wires and the rulers. They first laid out the
general form with wooden beams covered with lath work.
The wood was then covered with a coating of plaster.
They verified the large measurements already established,
and then executed the reproduction point by point, and
finished the modeling of the surfaces. Each nail head and
point marked requires six measurements, three on the
model and three for the enlargement without counting the

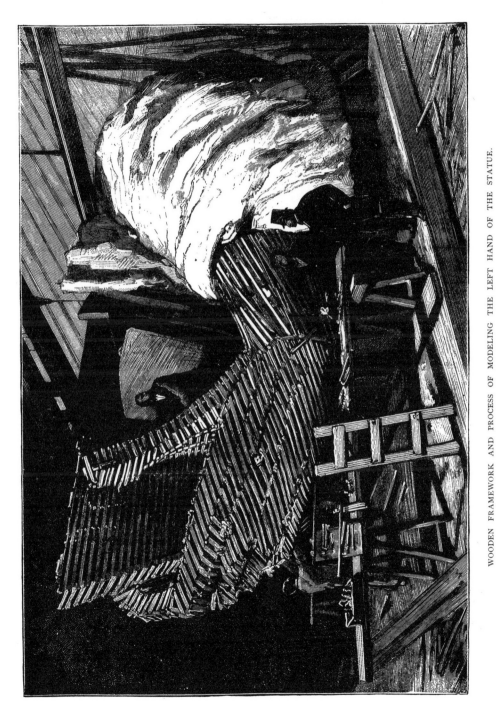

WOODEN FRAMEWORK AND PROCESS OF MODELING THE LEFT HAND OF THE STATUE.
From *Harper's Weekly*, Jan. 6th, 1883.

verifying measurements. There were in each course about 300 large points and more than 1,200 secondary points, which represented for each course, the work of establishing about 9,000 measurements. When a course was finished the carpenters took its forms by means of boards cut in profile, according to the form of the plaster. They were applied on the spot, placed one opposite to another and crossed, thus forming pigeon-holes, larger or smaller. Thus they took a sort of impression. In these wooden moulds or " gabarits," the hammers pressed the sheets of copper by pressure with levers, and by hammering with mallets. The pieces of copper were finished by beating them with little hammers and with rammers. The profile of the forms was again taken in detail with sheets of lead, pressed upon the model, again working the copper according to the profiles. The pieces of copper were furnished from point to point with iron braces, intended to give them rigidity. These braces were forged in the form of the copper when the contour of the latter was completely modeled. Thus furnished, the pieces were carried to the mounting in the court, to be brought together and fastened on the powerful trusswork of iron beams which serves as support for the whole envelope of the statue. The core of this trusswork is formed by a sort of pylon which has four points of attachment. Each of these points is sustained by three bolted braces, fifteen centimetres in diameter, which are made fast at a depth of eight metres in the masonry of the foundation to a frame of iron beams. The whole truss-work was designed and executed by the eminent constructing engineer, M. Eiffel.

SHAPING A SHEET OF COPPER ON THE MOULD.
From *Le Monde Illustre.*

This trusswork serves as a support for the copper form of the statue. The copper plates, kept in shape by iron bands, are supported by iron braces, which are cramped on to the central core. They do not bear in the least

PREPARING TO TAKE THE STATUE TO PIECES.
From *St. Nicholas*, July, 1884.

upon the lower plates, and their weight is always inde-
pendent of all that is above and below. [See illustration
Note E.]

Exhaustive mathematical calculations were made upon the resisting power of the iron pieces, upon the centre of gravity and upon the action of high winds. The calculations were made by taking as a base the most powerful hurricanes which have been recorded either in America or in Europe. In regard to the preservation of the work, since all the elements of its construction are everywhere visible on the inside in all their details, it will be easily kept in good condition.

To end this account, I ought to add to it a few bits of statistical information, although they have been published on various occasions. The whole work was done in the celebrated house of Gaget, Gauthier & Co., of Paris. The statue is constructed of copper sheets, two and a half millimetres in thickness. It measures 46.08 metres from the base to the top of the torch, 35.50 metres from below the plinth to the crown, 34 metres from the heel to the top of the head.*

The forefinger is 2.45 metres in length, and 1.44 metres in circumference at the second joint. The nail measures .35 metres by .26 metres. The head is 4.40 metres in height. The eye is .65 metres in width. The nose is

---

* The complete English measurement is as follows : From bottom of plinth to top of tower, 151 feet, 1 inch ; height of bottom foundation of pedestal above low water, 13 feet ; height of foundation mass, 52 feet, 10 inches ; height of pedestal proper, 89 feet ; total height of top of torch above low water mark, 305 feet, 11 inches.

1.12 metres in length. About forty persons were accommodated in the head at the Universal Exposition of 1878. It is possible to ascend into the torch above the hand. It will easily hold twelve persons. The total weight is about 200,000 kilos, of which 80,000 are copper and 120,000 iron. It represents an outlay of more than a million francs, including gifts, gratuitous work and the losses of all those who gave their devoted assistance to the work.

The colossal statues which have been executed up to the present time are far from the proportions of the Statue of Liberty. (See notes). Yet we must not expect its appearance to be colossal when it is in its place. In the immense picture which will surround it, it will appear simply in harmony with the whole, and have the normal aspect of a statue in a public place. It should be thus, because its part is not to appear extraordinary in itself, but to connect itself intimately with an extraordinary whole.

The statue was born for this place which inspired its conception. May God be pleased to bless my efforts and my work, and to crown it with the success, the duration and the moral influence which it ought to have. I shall be happy to have been able to consecrate the best years of my life to being the interpreter of the noble hearts whose dream has been the realization of the monument to the French-American Union. BARTHOLDI.

[NOTE A.]

The appeal which was issued to the public in 1875 by the promoters and organizers of the French-American Union was expressed as follows :

America is soon to celebrate the hundredth anniversary of her independence. That date marks an epoch in the history of humanity : to the New World, it recalls her work, the foundation of the great Republic ; to France, one of the most honorable pages in her history.

In concert with our friends in the United States we think this is a befitting occasion for associating France and America in a common demonstration. In spite of the lapse of time, the United States love to recall our ancient fraternity in arms ; always among them the name of France is held in honor. The great event which is to be celebrated on the Fourth of July, 1876, allows us to celebrate with our American brothers the old and strong friendship which for a long time has united the two peoples.

The New World is preparing to give extraordinary splendor to that festival ; friends of the United States have thought that the genius of France ought to display itself in a dazzling form. A French artist has embodied that thought in a plan worthy of its object, and which is approved by all ; he has come to an understanding with our friends in America, and has prepared all the means for executing the plan.

It is proposed to erect, as a memorial of the glorious anniversary, an exceptional monument. In the midst of the harbor of New York, upon an islet which belongs to the Union of the States, in front of Long Island, where was poured out the first blood for independence, a colossal statue would rear its head, outlined upon space, framed on the horizon by the great American cities of New York, Jersey City and Brooklyn. At the threshold of that vast continent, full of a new life, where arrive all the vessels of the world, the statue will rise upon the bosom of the waves. It will represent " Liberty Enlightening the World." At night a resplendent aureole upon its brow will throw its beams far upon the vast sea.

That monument will be executed in common by the two peoples, associated in this fraternal work as they were of old in founding independence. We will make a gift of the statue to our friends in America; they will unite with us in meeting the expenses of the execution and of the erection of the monument, which will serve as a pedestal.

We will in this way declare by an imperishable memorial the friendship that the blood spilled by our fathers sealed of old between the two nations.

Let us unite in the celebration of this festival of modern peoples. It is necessary for us to be numerous in order to give to that demonstration the brilliancy that it ought to have that it may be worthy of the past. Let us each bring his mite. The smallest subscriptions will be heartily welcomed. Let the number of signers testify to the sentiments of France.

The principal signers to that appeal were : Messieurs Laboulaye, De Noailles, De Rémusat, Waddington, Henri Martin, De Rochambeau, Dietz Mounir, De Tocqueville, O. de Lafayette, De Lasteyrie, Count Sérurier, Volowski and others.

————

[NOTE B.]

A sub-committee of this general committee, consisting of Messrs. Wm. M. Evarts, Ex-Gov. E. D. Morgan, Parke Godwin, Clarke Bell and J. W. Pinchot, was charged with the duty of procuring the necessary legislation, and obtained from Congress, on the recommendation of President Hayes, the passage of the following joint resolution :

Joint Resolution, authorizing the President to designate and set apart a site for the colossal statue of " Liberty Enlightening the World," and to provide for the permanent maintenance and preservation thereof.

Whereas, The President has communicated to Congress the information that citizens of the French Republic propose to commemorate the one hundredth anniversary of our independence by erecting, at their own cost, a colossal bronze statue of "Liberty Enlightening the World," upon a pedestal of suitable proportions, to be built by private subscription, upon one of the islands belonging to the United States in the harbor of New York; and

Whereas, It is proper to provide for the care and preservation of this grand monument of art, and of the abiding friendship of our ancient ally; therefore, be it

Resolved, By the Senate and House of Representatives of the United States of America in Congress assembled, that the President of the United States be and he is hereby authorized and directed to accept the colossal statue of "Liberty Enlightening the World," when presented by citizens of the French Republic, and to designate and set apart for the erection thereof a suitable site upon either Governor's or Bedloe's Island, in the harbor of New York; and upon the completion thereof shall cause the same to be inaugurated with such ceremonies as will serve to testify the gratitude of our people for this expressive and felicitous memorial of the sympathy of the citizens of our sister Republic; and he is hereby authorized to cause suitable regulations to be made for its future maintenance as a beacon, and for the permanent care and preservation thereof as a monument of art, and of the continued good will of the great nation which aided us in our struggle for freedom.

[Note C.]

M. Henri Martin having offered a toast to the Republic of the United States and to President Grant, Mr. Washburne responded in English to the toast with a remarkable address delivered extempore, which was happily received. Following are some extracts :

I must avow that there is here in the atmosphere this evening such a sentiment of cordial friendship and international fraternity, that it would be difficult for me to keep silence and not give vent to the emotion with which I am filled. There is in truth something touching, something which transports us, in that magnificent conception of the French people, of the erection upon the shores of America of a monument coming from the skilful hands of your remarkable artist, M. Bartholdi, which will recall the hundredth anniversary of the independence of my country, and which will be the lasting evidence of that ancient friendship between France and the American colonies, that has been sealed by the best blood of the two peoples. [Hearty applause.]

The work, the initiative in which was taken here by France in that fraternal spirit that fills us, all of us Americans, with pride and with gratitude, will find an echo in the homes of all our fellow-countrymen on the other side of the Atlantic. [Applause.]

The names of your illustrious fellow-countrymen will always be dear to the memory and to the heart of the American people. With what joy have my fellow-countrymen been able here this evening to congratulate themselves upon the presence of the grandsons of Lafayette, of Rochambeau, of Bouille. Our hearts and our hands have gone out to them in grateful acknowledgment, in remembrance of the services which their ancestors rendered to my country. [Long continued applause.]

Never, gentlemen, will my fellow-countrymen forget the courage, the perseverance and the sufferings of those French private soldiers, who fought side by side, shoulder to shoulder with the American soldiers, and poured out their generous blood for the defence of our liberties. Their ashes have remained mingled with our soil upon those memorable fields of battle that they had already reddened with their blood. May the turf grow more green and the wild flower bloom more beautifully upon their unknown tomb. [Redoubled applause.]

—

The beginning and the close of the remarkable address of M. Laboulaye, which was a model of eloquence and of patriotism, was as follows :

GENTLEMEN : We are assembled this evening to celebrate and to cement the friendship which unites France and America. That friendship is of very old date, and when next year on the Fourth of July America will signalize by a festival the anniversary of her Declaration of Independence, she will celebrate at the same time the anniversary of her alliance with France. [Cries of ''Good,'' ''Good.'']

As for you, gentlemen, who come from America, and whom we have the happiness of possessing this evening ; you, who have expressed yourselves so nobly by the mouth of your honorable Minister, take back to your country that which you have seen and heard ; say to your fellow-citizens that France always remains faithful to America.

To-day other peoples more happy, more stirring, may attempt to dispute with us your affection ; but recall to mind that when you were feeble and abandoned, France took with a warm pressure the hand that you held out to her. [Prolonged applause.]

In a century the centenary of independence will be celebrated again. We shall then be only forgotten dust. America, who will then have more than a hundred millions of inhabitants will be ignorant of our names. But this statue will remain. It will be the memorial of this festival, the visible proof of our affection. Symbol of a friendship which braves the storms of time, it will stand there unshaken in the midst of the winds which will roar around its head and the waves which will shatter their fury at its feet. [Applause.]

[Note D.]

Official presentation of the work of the French-American Union to His Excellency the Minister of the United States, July 4, 1884.

THE STATUE OF LIBERTY.—On Friday, July 4th, on the occasion of the anniversary of the Declaration of Independence of the United States, M. Ferdinand de Lesseps, President of the American-Union, officially presented at Paris the statue of "Liberty Enlightening the World" to Mr. Levi Morton, Minister of the United States. As early as 10 o'clock the workshops of the constructors were besieged by the crowd, and a number of curious persons had perched themselves on the roofs of the neighboring houses. The whole establishment was dressed with the French and American colors. At 11 o'clock, heralded by "The Marseillaise," the official cortege took its place under a pavilion erected for the occasion. M. Ferdinand de Lesseps opened the speaking, and read the following letter from M. Jules Ferry, who was not able to be present at the ceremony :

"PARIS, July 4, 1884.

"MY DEAR MR. MORTON :

"As you perhaps know, I have been seriously sick, and to fulfil all my duties I am obliged to take precautions to which I am hardly accustomed. Yesterday's work greatly fatigued me, and for to-day I am ordered to take a complete rest. The Government of the Republic will be represented in your presence by several Ministers. It is my loss and my regret that I am unable to be present at this festival of the fraternity of the two great Republics. But you know that I shall be there in spirit, in heart and in soul.

"Believe, my dear Mr. Morton, in my entire devotion,

JULES FERRY."

Then M. de Lesseps, after an allusion to the Panama Canal, "which is the work of the citizens of the two Republics," thanked M. Bartholdi, who conceived and executed the immense statue, which may be characterized, said he, as the eighth wonder of the world. M. de Lesseps said that he was handing over to the United States this great artistic monument, the gift of France, to which have contributed by their votes 180 cities, forty general councils, a large number of chambers of commerce and of societies, and over a hundred thousand subscribers. He thanked the modest co-workers, M. Bergeret, M. Baron, and particularly M. Simon, the brave assistant of M. Bartholdi. He dwelt upon the merit of the great industrial house, Gaget, Gauthier & Co., whose director, M. Gaget, was able so successfully to accomplish such extraordinary labors. He concluded by saying :

"This work, Mr. Minister, is the product of enthusiasm, of devotion, of intelligence, and of the noblest sentiments which can animate man. It is great in its conception and in its realization. It is colossal in its proportions, and we hope that it will grow still greater through its moral worth, thanks to the remembrances and the sentiments which it is to perpetuate. We commit it to your care, Mr. Minister, that it may remain forever the pledge of the bonds which should unite France and the great American nation."

Mr. Morton then answered M. de Lesseps by reading a congratulatory telegram from the President of the United States. He eulogized M. Bartholdi and his co-workers, and warmly thanked France for this new testimony of friendship, which owed its beginning to the people. He concluded by thanking Admiral Peyron, who had offered a vessel for the transportation of the statue.

After this speech M. de Lesseps requested the Ministers to sign the deed of gift, a magnificent parchment enveloped in a case of Russian leather, of which the text is as follows :

"OFFICIAL REPORT OF THE PRESENTATION OF THE STATUE TO THE MINISTER OF THE UNITED STATES.

"In the year one thousand eight hundred and eighty-four, the fourth day of July, being the anniversary of the Independence of the United States.

8

" In the presence of M. Jules Ferry, President of the Council of Ministers, Minister of Foreign Affairs ; Count Ferdinand de Lesseps, in the name of the Committee of the French-American work, and of the national demonstration of which the committee has been the organ, presented the colossal statue of "Liberty Enlightening the World," the work of the sculptor M. Bartholdi, to His Excellency Mr. Morton, Minister Plenipotentiary of the United States, requesting him to be the mouth-piece of the national sentiment of which this work is the expression.

" Mr. Morton, in the name of his countrymen, thanks the French-American Union for this testimony of the sympathy of the French nation. He declares that by virtue of the powers conferred upon him by the President of the United States and by the Committee of the work in America, represented by its honorable president, Mr. William M. Evarts, he accepts the statue, and that it will be erected, in conformity with the vote of Congress on February 22, 1877, in the harbor at New York, in memory of the century-old friendship between the two nations.

" In testimony whereof we have hereunto set our hands.

" In the name of France.—JULES FERRY.

" In the name of the United States.—MORTON.

" BRISSON, President of the Chamber.

" In the name of the Committee of the French-American Union.

FERDINAND DE LESSEPS.

E. DE LAFAYETTE."

While the trumpets played " The Marseillaise," the guests grouped themselves in front of the statue, the torch of which was adorned with flags.

The Liberty is the largest work of its kind that has ever been completed. The famous Colossus of Rhodes, according to the proportions which the legends attribute to it, was but a miniature in comparison. The other reputedly immense statues are also quite small beside this gigantic copper figure. Thus the Bavaria at Munich measures fifteen metres, seventy centimetres; the Virgin of Puy, sixteen metres; Arminius, twenty-eight metres; St. Charles Borromeo, twenty-two metres. The Column Vendome is only forty-four metres in height, and "Liberty Enlightening the World" measures forty-six metres from the base to the top of the torch.

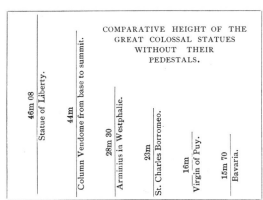

COMPARATIVE HEIGHT OF THE GREAT COLOSSAL STATUES WITHOUT THEIR PEDESTALS.

46m 08 Statue of Liberty.

44m Column Vendome from base to summit.

28m 30 Arminius in Westphalie.

23m St. Charles Borromeo.

16m Virgin of Puy.

15m 70 Bavaria.

Scale of 1 millimetre to the metre.

STATUE OF LIBERTY. ST. CHARLES BORROMEO. VIRGIN OF PUY. BAVARIA.

[Note E.]

The following description of the pedestal of the statue is from " Harper's Weekly " of June 6th :

The pedestal designed by Mr. M. R. Hunt for Bartholdi's statue of "Liberty Enlightening the World," which is built inside the stone walls of the fort on Bedloe's Island, is worthy of the great figure that will stand on it. Architecturally it is, as it ought to be, not obtrusive in design or ornamentation, but its massiveness is sufficiently relieved by architectural variety and ornament to prevent an appearance of a mere pyramid of stone. The design is such that the pedestal calls no attention to itself, but directs it to the statue ; and so modest is it in its appearance that a spectator would not be likely to guess how large and how high it is.

The foundation of the pedestal proper is 91 feet square at its base, and 66 feet 7 inches square at the top. It makes its pyramidal ascent, not with a continuous wall, but with a series of great layers of concrete, each one smaller than the one it rests on. The base of this foundation mass is 13 feet above the mean low-water mark, and its top 52 feet 10 inches. The pedestal, itself, therefore, begins at an elevation of 65 feet 10 inches, which is high above the stone walls of the fort. From these walls curved footways lead to the top of the foundation at the centre of every side. Every side of the foundation and of the pedestal is alike. The solidity of this vast foundation work is broken only by wide passage-ways through it at a level with the ground, and a circular vertical shaft in the middle, up which stairways and an elevator will run.

At its base the pedestal proper is 62 feet square. In the centre of each side, at the base, is a doorway 5 feet wide and 13 feet high in the middle, to which the footways from the walls of the fort ascend. On either side of every door is a projecting disk of stone, on which will be placed the coats of arms of France and the United States in relief. A good architectural effect is produced by the rough-stone work at the corners of the pedestal. Above the doors there are on every side ten projecting stone disks, which, though they are 4 feet 6 inches in diameter, appear almost

THE PEDESTAL AS IT NOW APPEARS, SHOWING ITS UNFINISHED STATE.

From *Harper's Weekly*, June 6, 1885.

as small as mere bead-work to a spectator standing on the ground. On these the coats of arms of the States of the Union will be placed in relief.

This is the line that has now been reached in construction; above it the more elaborate superstructure begins. Above the disks are large panels 23 feet 6 inches long and 5 feet 3 inches high, on which there will be appropriate inscriptions and designs. At an elevation of 72 feet 8 inches the walls of the pedestal are to recede, leaving on every side between them and two large columns and two pilasters a balcony on which doors from the inside open. This balcony is 5 feet 8 inches in width, and extends along the wall from corner pillar to corner pillar. The view from the balcony, on one side, of New York City, Brooklyn, Governor's Island, New Jersey, and the East River Bridge, and on the other, of Staten Island and the Bay—will be among the finest that can be enjoyed anywhere in the vicinity of New York.

Above these pillars the pedestal becomes smaller, and its upper platform is 39 feet 4⅜ inches square. By reason of the steps on the sides of the foundation, the doors in the lower part of the pedestal, the pediments, the projecting stone disks, the panels and the balcony, what would otherwise have been the monotonous walls of a pyramid, have been relieved so as to produce a good architectural effect, and at the same time to give the appearance of the great elevation to the statue itself, and not to the pedestal. On this surface, nearly forty feet square, the gigantic statue will stand, its footstool 89 feet above the mean low-water mark. The statue is 151 feet 1 inch high, and the top of the torch will be at an elevation of 305 feet 11 inches from mean low-water mark.

The ground was first broken for the erection of the pedestal in April, 1883; the excavation was begun in June; the laying of the foundation in October; and work was continued until December, 1884—a period of eighteen months. Work was again begun on May 11, 1885, and the work will not be completed before it will have required nearly two years of continuous labor of as many men as can work on it. The stone is from a quarry on Leete's Island in Connecticut, and the whiteness of the rough quoins gives a pleasant effect at a distance of several

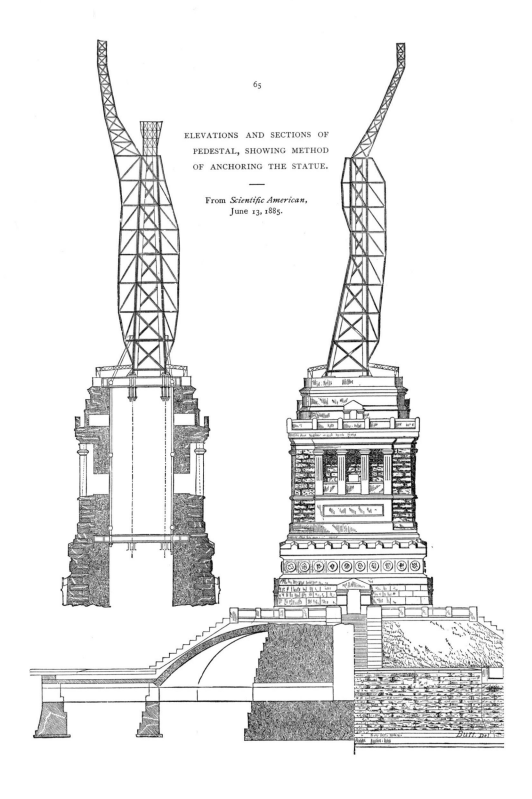

ELEVATIONS AND SECTIONS OF
PEDESTAL, SHOWING METHOD
OF ANCHORING THE STATUE.

—

From *Scientific American,*
June 13, 1885.

miles. These quoins are so heavy that the labor of lifting them to such a height has made the building of the pedestal one of the heaviest pieces of masonry ever done, even in the vicinity of New York, where the piers of the East River Bridge stand as monuments of massive stone work. The total cost will not be less than $250,000.

Colonel Charles P. Stone, the engineer-in-chief, has as large a force of men as can work on the structure at once, and it will be finished as rapidly as possible. The pedestal has been built to stand for all time to come.

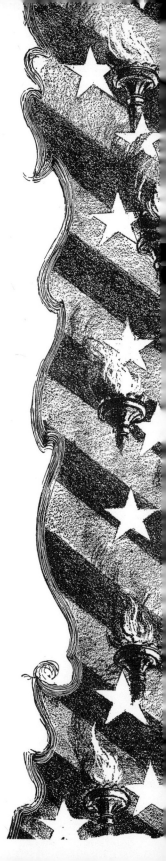

PRICE 75 CENTS